ESTRENO Collection of Contemporary Spanish Plays

General Editor: Phyllis Zatlin

KILLING TIME

and

KEEPING IN TOUCH

ESTRENO CONTEMPORARY SPANISH PLAYS

General Editor

Phyllis Zatlin
Professor of Spanish
Rutgers, The State University

Advisory Board

Sharon Carnicke
Professor of Theatre and
Associate Dean
University of Southern California

Martha Halsey
Professor of Spanish
Penn State University

Sandra Harper
Editor, *Estreno*
Ohio Wesleyan University

Marion Peter Holt
Critic and Translator
New York City

Steven Hunt
Associate Professor of Theatre
Converse College

Felicia Hardison Londré
Curators' Professor of Theatre
University of Missouri-Kansas City
American Theatre Fellow

Christopher Mack
Writer and Director
Paris

Grant McKenie
Professor of Theatre
University of Oregon

BETH ESCUDÉ I GALLÈS

KILLING TIME
(*El color del gos quan fuig*)

Translated from the Catalan
by
Bethany M. Korp

KEEPING IN TOUCH
(*La lladre i la Sra Guix*)

Translated from the Catalan
by
Janet DeCesaris

ESTRENO Plays
New Brunswick, New Jersey
2003

ESTRENO Contemporary Spanish Plays 23
General Editor: Phyllis Zatlin
105 George Street, New Brunswick, New Jersey
Rutgers, The State University of New Jersey 08901-1414 USA

Library of Congress Cataloging in Publication Data
Escudé i Gallès, Beth, 1963-
  Killing Time and Keeping in Touch
  Bibliography:
  Contents: Killing Time. Keeping in Touch.
Translations of: El color del gos quan fuig. La lladre i la Sra Guix.
  1. Escudé i Gallès, Beth, 1963-
      Translation, English.
I. Korp, Bethany M. and DeCesaris, Janet. II. Title.
Library of Congress Control No.: 2002112275
ISBN: 1-888463-15-5

Published with support from
Institució de les Lletres Catalanes

Cover: Jeffrey Eads

TABLE OF CONTENTS

BETH ESCUDÉ I GALLÈS
Photo by Phyllis Zatlin

ABOUT THE PLAYWRIGHT

Born in Barcelona in 1963, Beth Escudé i Gallès holds a degree in stage direction and drama from the Theatre Institute in Barcelona. She has also studied playwrighting at the Royal Court Theatre of London and with José Sanchis Sinisterra. She teaches set design and visual communication at the Universitat Politècnica in València and drama and dramaturgy at the Theatre Institute in Barcelona. She also collaborates with such companies as La Fura dels Baus, Nats Nus, S. P. Producions and Nessum Dorma as director and dramaturg.

Escudé's first text, *El destí de les violetes* (*The Destiny of Violets*, 1995) uses a structural game that exposes eight different possible lives for the main character. The choice of each different life path gives way to a new character, a new Violet. Escudé playfully assigns the characters a destiny they cannot escape. *El pensament per enemic* (*If I Were You*, 1996), presents the story of two criminals who kidnap a young woman that is never present on stage. The play inverts and distorts the conventional values attached to violence, fidelity, love and cruelty in pursuit of "turning into poetry what cannot be poetry and regarding everyday life as sacred," in Escudé's own words. Like *El destí de les violetes*, the play looks into the multiplicity of life possibilities and the implications of past decisions. The adult woman and marginalized male characters in *If I Were You* share an underworld that finds its ultimate expression in their own words and games. Through these games, the characters are able to exchange personalities with no further implications (thus the English title provided by John London for the Royal Court Theatre staging).

El color del gos quan fuig (Killing Time) explores the story of a young woman and her mother-in-law who resort to mythology and literature, taking whatever suits them in order to explain their existence. It is an intertextual piece by its exposure of the recreation of life through fiction in a highly poetic language. This intertextuality encompasses the postmodern mixture of high registers (the Bible, Greek tragedy) and low registers of "supermarket poetics," as Sanchis Sinisterra defines Escudé's style. Other works by Escudé include *Les nenes mortes no creixen* (*Dead Girls Don't Grow Up*, Joaquim Bartrina Prize, 2001), *Beats* (*The Blessed*, Tricicle Prize, 2002), short plays like *¿Ciudadano qué?* (*Citizen K-what?*), written with Alejandro Montiel, and *La lladre i la Sra Guix* (*Keeping in Touch*). These plays deal with such diverse topics as the difficulty of family relationships, loneliness in the city, the tragicomedy of an art robbery, immigration, and cinematography. Taken as a group, they define Escudé as a distinctive voice in the new generation of Catalan playwrights.

Eulàlia Borràs Riba
EUETII—Universitat Politècnica de Catalunya

A NOTE ON THE PLAYS

It has been said that one difference between a novel and a short story is that a novel can use a world to describe a single event whereas a short story uses a single event to illuminate an entire world. The same could be said of the short play format. In the two one-act plays contained in this volume (*Killing Time* and *Keeping in Touch*), Beth Escudé i Gallès does just that. In both plays, we are introduced to characters whose names are as generic as YOUNG WOMAN and OLD WOMAN. On the surface both plays deal with somewhat everyday events and relationships. In *Killing Time,* a mother and daughter-in-law deal with their lives after the death of the son/husband, and in *Keeping in Touch,* a victim of a purse robbery contacts the thief through her stolen cell phone. But Escudé i Gallès uses these situations as windows to explore the nature of humanness in ways that are as enlightening as they are profound. What results are short plays that possess richness, complexity and depth.

Towards the end of *Killing Time,* the YOUNG WOMAN gives a massage to her mother-in-law as she quotes from the last of many stories they have shared. "Every day Chandra would be thrilled to receive Draupadi's caresses, and every day Chandra would give Draupadi an old story, a story of love or loss that had to do with the two of them." And it is here that we get a sense of how these two characters have, up to now, lived—by "killing time" telling stories. But there is something underneath, something painful in the jealousy and resentment that lies below the surface. Earlier in the play we find out that the OLD WOMAN is leaving, presumably to a home for the elderly. But as the play progresses we become more and more aware of what is really happening. And by the end, although we may be shocked, ultimately we are not surprised at the outcome. Escudé i Gallès does more than just relate a story about these two women, though. By weaving in and out references to mythological characters such as Naomi and Ruth, Andromache and Hecuba, as well as Draupadi and Chandra, she connects to a universality that relates to women across many cultures and times.

In *Keeping in Touch*, we are again introduced to characters named "YOUNG and OLD WOMAN," though they are quite different. After a purse robbery, we find out that amid the contents of make-up and money that the YOUNG WOMAN has stolen, the one object the OLD WOMAN wants back is an old worn photograph—the last image she has of her deceased father and herself. When the YOUNG WOMAN says she can't return it but instead will describe it over the phone, the OLD WOMAN has no choice but to visualize what she thought had been so familiar to her. She then starts to "see" things in the photo never before seen. As much as the OLD WOMAN needs to hear about the photo, the YOUNG WOMAN needs someone with whom she can share her life, her frustrations and struggles that come with being an immigrant in a new land. We then become witnesses to a startling new relationship between strangers that strikes a surprisingly familiar chord with all of us. At the same time, we encounter not only the unexpected stranger we meet but also the stranger inside ourselves.

In both *Killing Time* and *Keeping in Touch*, Escudé i Gallès provides snapshots into the complex worlds of her characters. And like short stories, these two brief plays are able to capture insightful images of a vaster universe.

Steven Hunt
Associate Professor of Theatre
Department of Theatre and Dance
Converse College
Spartanburg, South Carolina

Inquiries regarding permissions should be addressed to the author through

D. Alfredo Carrión Saiz
Director de Artes Escénicas y Musicales
Sociedad General de Autores y Editores
Fernando VI, 4
28004 Madrid, SPAIN
Phone: 011-34-91-349-96-86   Fax: 011-34-91-349-97-12
E-mail: acarrion@sgae.es

or through the translators:

Janet DeCesaris
Facultat de Traducció i Interpretació
Universitat Pompeu Fabra
Rambla, 30-32
08002 Barcelona, SPAIN
Phone: 011-34-93-542-2248   Fax: 011-34-93-542-1617

Bethany M. Korp
186 Ocean Avenue
Laurence Harbor, NJ 08879
Phone: 1-732-566-0458, 1-732-991-5861
E-mail: bmkorp@hotmail.com

xiii

KILLING TIME
(El color del gos quan fuig)

Translated from the Catalan

by

Bethany M. Korp

El color del gos quan fuig (Killing Time) was first performed as a staged reading at the Centre d'Estudis Catalans in Paris in April 1997, directed by Sonia Abella. It received its first stage production at the Sala Beckett in Barcelona in May 1997, under the direction of Beth Escudé i Gallès.

The Castilian translation by Alejandro Montiel Mues, *Pullus (El resplandor del lomo en las liebres huidizas)*, was first performed in Buenos Aires in October 2000 at Teatro del Sur (dir. Ricardo Holcer), and received its Spanish premiere at Madrid's Sala Galileo in September 2001, under the direction of Adolfo Simón.

El color del gos quan fuig has also been performed in French (*Entre chien et loup*, translated by Isabelle Bres) at the Catalan Studies Center in Paris in March 2000 (dir. Miguel Sevilla) and at the Théâtre Baudouin-Bunton in Brussels (dir. Véronika Mabardi, March 2000). The Italian version, *Il colore del canne quando fugge* (translated by Riccardo Rombi) was staged by Les Quayelles theatre company at the Festival Il Catello Sommerso in Florence.

CHARACTERS

OLD WOMAN (blind)
YOUNG WOMAN

The OLD WOMAN is seated in a chair, in her underwear, possibly in a robe. The YOUNG WOMAN enters with a paper bag that she sets down purposefully. Silence.

OLD WOMAN: Where were you?

YOUNG WOMAN: How did you get down to the dining room?

OLD WOMAN: I want to be ready when they get here. Have you packed my suitcase?

YOUNG WOMAN: By yourself? Did you come down by yourself?

OLD WOMAN: You weren't here. I wanted to be ready when they come to get me. You weren't here. I couldn't hear you mopping. (*Laughs.*) You weren't here. I heard you wake up. Early. Very early. Too early. I heard you open your eyes. (*Imitates the sound of eyes opening.*) I heard you tiptoe down the stairs. You were thinking too quietly to be heard. (*Laughs.*) I couldn't figure out where you were going or why you had gotten up so early. You were thinking too quietly. Maybe tomorrow I'll hear what you think. (*Laughs.*)

YOUNG WOMAN: Tomorrow you'll be too far away. (*Pause.*) Sorry. (*Pause.*)

OLD WOMAN: Have you packed my suitcase, Ruth?

YOUNG WOMAN: I haven't packed your suitcase because I already told you, you don't need a suitcase. And don't call me Ruth.

OLD WOMAN: Don't forget to put in the travel sewing kit. And my travel makeup case. And the travel iron. In the suitcase.

YOUNG WOMAN: You don't need any of that stuff. They give you everything there.

OLD WOMAN: And my neck pillow. That would be good. (*Pause.*) Come on, what are you waiting for? Fix my hair, give me my massage, dress me, let's get this over with.

YOUNG WOMAN: It's not time yet.

OLD WOMAN: When will it be time?

YOUNG WOMAN: Right now I have to mop. And I haven't cleaned your toilet yet.

OLD WOMAN: Even though you got up so early? (*Pause.*) When will it be time? In ten minutes, will it be time? (*Pause.*) I'm bored. (*Pause.*) That cat! Go tell old Agnes to make that damn cat shut up.

YOUNG WOMAN: I already did. But she told me that she can't hear him, he ran away a few days ago, she can't hear him anymore. (*Pause.*) She was very sad. She thinks he's dead.

OLD WOMAN: I wish. But he's not. He's running around, not too far from here. A hundred and forty yards. Maybe a hundred and thirty. (*Pause.*) I'm bored. (*Pause.*) The library! You little bandit! Did you go back to the library to steal stories? I knew it, Ruth, dear! You went out to steal a new story for me, a going-away present, one last story—

YOUNG WOMAN: No. I didn't go to the library. I don't want to steal any more stories. We swore we wouldn't do it anymore. I didn't go to the library. No. You swore, too. We swore to give them all back just like we found them. And don't call me Ruth. My name isn't Ruth.

OLD WOMAN: What do you want me to call you?

YOUNG WOMAN: My name.

(*Pause.*)

OLD WOMAN: We can't give them back. They're not whole. They're torn up, mutilated, perverted—

YOUNG WOMAN: disguised, summarized, falsified—

BOTH: massacred, mixed-up, wilted, spiced-up, added-to—

YOUNG WOMAN (*Cutting her off*): We'll try.

OLD WOMAN: All of them?

YOUNG WOMAN: All of them. Whole. Just like we found them.

OLD WOMAN: Can't we just keep ... one? Just one. One that I could take with me. The one we like best. Both of us. The one that's most ours. Don't deny me this little whim, now that you're throwing me out of my own house, eh, dear?

(*Silence.*)

YOUNG WOMAN: You'll be fine. There's a garden.

OLD WOMAN: And silence?

YOUNG WOMAN: A garden, and silence. Plenty of silence. You'll be fine. (*Pause.*) I dreamed last night.

OLD WOMAN: You dreamed? A story? Did you dream a story?

YOUNG WOMAN: A short one.

OLD WOMAN: Does it have anything to do with us?

YOUNG WOMAN: Yes.

OLD WOMAN: Some kind of drivel—

YOUNG WOMAN: No, it's not. It's not drivel at all.

OLD WOMAN: I'm sure. I know all about your dreams.

YOUNG WOMAN: Fine. Then I won't tell you about it. I have a lot of work to do.

OLD WOMAN: What work? Don't bother scrubbing the toilet for me, it doesn't matter anymore.

YOUNG WOMAN: I wasn't going to scrub the toilet right now. But look at this floor. Doesn't it sound dirty? What does that sound like? (*Tries to imitate the sound of a dirty floor when someone steps on it, but it is obvious that she is unsuccessful.*) I bought a product that will leave the floor like a mirror. You'll hear the sound of a mirror when you walk on it for the last time. Click-clank, swish, click-clank—

OLD WOMAN: Mopping, that's all you think about. I can't believe there are still people like you in this day and age. (*Pause.*) What are the names of the women in your stupid story?

YOUNG WOMAN: The daughter-in-law is Draupadi and the mother-in-law is Chandra.

OLD WOMAN: Exotic. You've dreamed up a stupid exotic story, drivel.

(*Pause.*)

YOUNG WOMAN: You want me to check your eyes?

OLD WOMAN: No. I don't have any eyes left, anymore. Last night I heard them rolling back into my head.

YOUNG WOMAN: Into your head? Let me see. (*The YOUNG WOMAN pushes up the OLD WOMAN's eyelids and examines her eye sockets closely.*) It looks like the disease is progressing ...

OLD WOMAN: Are they there?

YOUNG WOMAN: I see something yellowish, way in the back.

OLD WOMAN: I heard them rolling back, last night. They rolled back little by little, with great difficulty, scraping against the walls of the sockets. Now I can see the inside of my head. Nothing new. It's violet, like everything else. And it's the same raw violet color as the outside world. They rolled back little by little. Nothing stopped them from rolling back, but the walls were so dry!

YOUNG WOMAN: What was it like, the noise? Soft? Stretchy?

OLD WOMAN: You know I won't be able to describe it, curse you.

(*Pause.*)

YOUNG WOMAN: Did it hurt?

OLD WOMAN: Only the noise hurts. I don't feel the pain, just the damn noise and the pain of not being able to explain the noise. If only I could stop hearing how my body is breaking down, that would be something else entirely. If only I could put the details into words. Misfortune is lost in the details. (*Pause.*) I'm bored. Fix my hair, give me my massage, dress me, let's get this over with.

(*The YOUNG WOMAN picks up a brush wrapped in a silk handkerchief and fixes the OLD WOMAN'S hair. From time to time, the YOUNG WOMAN pulls out some of the OLD WOMAN'S hair without meaning to. The OLD WOMAN seems not to notice. The YOUNG WOMAN puts the hair in her pockets. Pause.*)

YOUNG WOMAN: "In the days when the judges judged, there was a famine in Palestine ..."

OLD WOMAN: What ... what are you doing?

YOUNG WOMAN: We have to give them all back.

OLD WOMAN: No. Not the one about Ruth and Naomi! I need that one. No. (*Cries.*)

YOUNG WOMAN: We don't have time, old woman. They're coming to get you. We don't have time. You're not making me believe you're crying, you don't have any tear ducts. I've seen. We have to give them all back. (*The OLD WOMAN stops whimpering.*) "In the days when the judges judged, there was a famine in Palestine. And thus Elimelech was forced to leave Bethlehem, his homeland, because of hunger. He took his wife, Naomi, and his two sons and went to the land of Moab, where they lived. Elimelech died, and Naomi married their two sons to women of Moab, Ruth and Orpah. And they dwelled there ten years. And the sons died also both of them, and Naomi was left alone in a strange land. Then she decided to return to her people, for she had heard the news that the Lord had turned his gaze again upon her homeland, feeding the people there. And thus Naomi went forth on the way to Bethlehem. When she saw that her two daughters-in-law went with her, she stopped and said:"

OLD WOMAN (*Mechanically*): "Go, return to your mother's house. The Lord have mercy on you, as ye have had on the dead and on me. The Lord grant you that ye have a happy life, each in the house of a new husband."

YOUNG WOMAN: "Then she kissed them. Orpah lifted up her voice and wept, and returned without looking back. But Ruth still clave to her."

OLD WOMAN (*Mechanically*): "Return, my daughter, why will ye go with me? Do not insist, it would grieve me too much to have you. The hand of the Lord is gone out against me." But you stayed with me, saying:

YOUNG WOMAN: "Whither thou goest, I will go. Where thou lodgest, I will lodge. Thy people are my people. Where thou diest, will I die, and there will I be buried."

OLD WOMAN: Steadfastly, the Moabitess insisted. It suited her to thus become a slave of her mother-in-law. Because Ruth was a virtuous woman, faithful, a little boring, fascinated by cleaning products, especially those that leave the floor like a mirror. She went crazy for those. Skweeky-Kleen. Liquid Superwax.

YOUNG WOMAN: No. We have to give them back just as they are! Don't tear them up, pervert them ...

OLD WOMAN: And I am returning it just as it is. Just as it has been.

YOUNG WOMAN: No. Don't confuse me. Not like it has been. Like it was.

OLD WOMAN: No. Besides, I don't want to give it back, not that one. We can't give it back, not that one. We would be left with nothing, stupid. Don't you realize that it would be as if we had never met? Today would make no sense. I wouldn't even be able to leave. And you want me to go, don't you? We need a story to begin, if we want to finish. We'll give back all the others. I swear. We'll be left with just two stories. Just two. The first and the last, eh, dear? Now, we just have to make up the last one. And don't try to pretend, I know my hair is falling out, even if I can't see it. (*The YOUNG WOMAN pulls hair out of her pockets and furtively throws it on the ground.*) We just have to make up the last one. We could even give back part of the story of Ruth. The part where you marry Boaz. It's really just drivel. We'll be left with the story up to that passage that's so pretty and so us, that says: "Ruth and Naomi arrived in Bethlehem. When they entered the city, everyone said ..." (*Pause.*)

YOUNG WOMAN (*Mechanically*): "Look, is this Naomi?"

OLD WOMAN: "Call me not Naomi, call me Mara, for the Almighty has filled me with bitterness. I went out full and I have returned empty." (*Pause.*) Up to there. The rest, away. We'll give it back to the books or whoever we have to give it back to. But let me take the name of Mara, the bitter one. It belongs to me as much as them. Don't take it from me.

(*Pause.*)

YOUNG WOMAN: But I was happy with Boaz. I like that passage, too.

OLD WOMAN: Bah. Drivel. If you want, you can keep the part where you were David's grandmother.

YOUNG WOMAN: No. I don't care about that. I ... I was happy with Boaz. I would rather not forget him.

OLD WOMAN: You see? You see how it's impossible to give them back, silly? (*Pause.*) What? Come on, give back your memory of Boaz. (*Pause.*) What? Should we give it back? (*Pause.*)

YOUNG WOMAN: Yes. I'll give it back. I'll give it back.

(*Brief pause.*)

OLD WOMAN: I'm bored. Is it time for my massage?

YOUNG WOMAN: No, not yet.

OLD WOMAN: What time is it?

YOUNG WOMAN: It's time for tea. We have to give back the rest; there are others to give back.

OLD WOMAN: Does it have a garden? (*Pause.*) A garden. Does it have one?

YOUNG WOMAN: Does it ever! I can remember it well. I remember the garden. Very pretty. With gravel. The ground is covered with gravel.

OLD WOMAN: It makes noise. (*Pause.*) It makes noise when you walk. You don't always feel like hearing the sound of gravel when you walk. Maybe you want to walk and just walk. Not walk and be accompanied by the sound of some damn gravel.

YOUNG WOMAN: And fireflies in the evening. It's all full of fireflies. Fireflies don't make noise.

OLD WOMAN: A lot of them?

YOUNG WOMAN: Tons. It's full of them.

OLD WOMAN: Then they will make noise, a ton of fireflies.

YOUNG WOMAN: No. They express themselves with words of light, fireflies do. (*Pause.*) You'll be fine. And you won't have to scrub the toilet. They cook your dinner, make your bed, and clean the toilet inside and out, every day.

OLD WOMAN: Mmm. (*Pause.*) Old Agnes told me that they give you butter cookies in the afternoon. Is that true? That they seem like homemade, but they're not, they're Danish, the ones that come in the blue tins. (*Pause.*) Then again, I don't know how the hell Agnes would know that about the snack. She's never been there! Lies. She's been getting older every year. Old Agnes said to me, "You're so blessed; in your old age, the Lord has given your soul a daughter-in-law who cares for you and is worth more than seven sons." Always spouting off with fucking religion. And she said that she still doesn't have the violet disease. That she can still see the other colors, that her eyes still see shapes. What a lie. It's perfectly clear that she's in the last stages. Yesterday, yes, yesterday I clearly heard a dry tear drop into her instant decaf café au lait. (*Imitates the sound of a dry tear dropping into an instant decaf café au lait. Pause.*) It will be hard for me to get used to it. I won't like it. I don't want to go there. Don't make me go. All full of old people. Old people complaining and telling lies all day. And in the afternoon, an old-person silence, I'll hear the grinding of their rotting teeth, I know it, I'll hear how their teeth come loose from their gums, how the teeth fall from their gums on their pillows, from the pillow to the sheet, and from the sheet, they fall onto the floor. Isn't it enough that I have to listen to my rotting teeth—and old Agnes's—without listening to hundreds of old people? The sound of gravel reminds me strongly of the sound of teeth. And in the morning I will walk through a garden covered with teeth.

YOUNG WOMAN: You'll have someone to talk to.

OLD WOMAN: Yes. About brands of drops for old people's dry eyes, brands of glue for old people's dentures ...

YOUNG WOMAN: The landscape is beautiful. Someone will describe the landscape to you ...

OLD WOMAN: They won't have to, I can imagine it: cancer in the distance, deserted pubes, rich rivers of incontinence. A magnificent landscape.

YOUNG WOMAN: If you don't like it with the others, you can go to your room—

OLD WOMAN: A single room.

YOUNG WOMAN: Maybe not at the beginning. But if there's a free one, I'm sure they'll put you in it.

OLD WOMAN: And how do you think it could empty? It's never empty, it always fills up. Hundreds of old people and their dentures arrive every day and they go straight into the rooms. How could a place like that be empty? Tell me, stupid, what is the reason that a place like that would be empty? Tell me! You don't go there to die, you're already dead when you get there. You go there to rot, if there's anything left to rot.

YOUNG WOMAN: No. No. They keep building more wings and when people arrive, they put them there. I'm sure it's possible that there are single rooms.

(*Pause.*)

OLD WOMAN: Oh. All right. So then I want a single. You hear? (*Pause.*) What could you hear, anyway! Old Agnes's cat is running through the woods—

YOUNG WOMAN: Really? I'll go tell her!

OLD WOMAN: Don't. (*Pause.*) He's running away. He's hiding. (*Pause.*) He's heading straight for the stream. Maybe he'll go under. Wait. (*Pause. Imitates the sound of a cat going underwater.*) A-ha! Poof! Did you hear it? (*Imitates the sound of a cat that has drowned. Laughs.*)

YOUNG WOMAN: You're cruel. Poor old Agnes.

OLD WOMAN (*Laughs*): And you're talking about cruelty? You, the one who's forcing me to leave my house? You, who out of pity is trying to hide my hair in your pockets as it falls out? (*Pause.*) Sweetheart, daughter, I won't know how

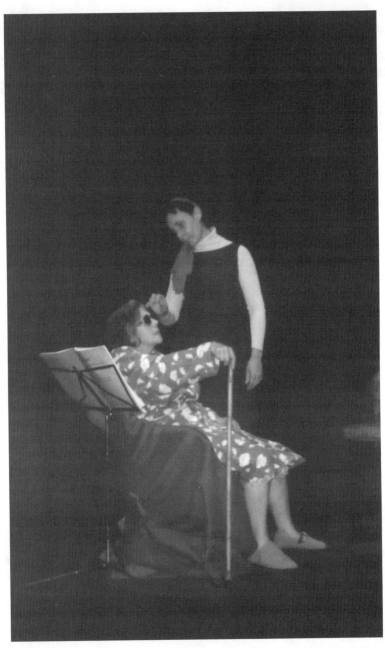

Pullus, el color del lomo de las liebres huidizas (Killing Time).
Teatro del Sur, Buenos Aires, October 2000, dir. Ricardo Holcer.

to be myself without you. Dear. (*The OLD WOMAN whimpers.*) I won't be able to feel alone, alone the way I feel when I'm with you. I don't want to go. Who will look out for me, for my eyes? I need you, you hear? I don't want to go.

YOUNG WOMAN: We can't go back. (*Pause.*) You have to go, you'll be better off than here, you know? They clean the toilet inside and out and they'll explain the color of the sunset aaaand I think that stuff about the snack is true, and, and they'll cure you: men with labcoats the color of sand will take care of you, they're specialists in the violet disease, and I ... I'll come see you soon, if you want, very soon, maybe ... "Whither thou goest, I will go."

OLD WOMAN (*Stops whimpering*): You don't need to. I can see perfectly well without your backward gaze. I will be free from having to listen to you mop the floor hour after hour and my footsteps against a mirrored floor. "Why the hell will ye come with me? May the Lord grant you happiness once and for fucking all with a new husband."

YOUNG WOMAN: I don't need a new husband. I was happy with your son, Mara.

OLD WOMAN: Don't call me Mara, call me Hecuba. (*Pause. The YOUNG WOMAN looks at her.*) What? We'll have to give back the story of Hecuba and Andromache, too, right? All of them. We have to give back all of them, dear. Your story of faithful love for Hector, too. My virtuous son and his exemplary wife. What's wrong, Andromache, girl? There we are. Don't call me Mara, call me Hecuba.

(*Long pause.*)

YOUNG WOMAN: It's time for your massage.

(*The YOUNG WOMAN undresses the OLD WOMAN very carefully.*)

OLD WOMAN: You hit my mesenteric vein.

YOUNG WOMAN: I'm sorry.

OLD WOMAN: Mmm. "Hector is dead, my daughter, your tears will not bring him back. Forget him. By these virtues that you hold dear, in which you take so much pride, try to please your new spouse." Uff. Now you've hit the other one.

YOUNG WOMAN: I'm sorry. (*Pause.*) I was happy with your son Hector, Hecuba. "I always did everything I could to be a perfect woman. I knew how to present myself before Hector with tranquil eyes and a silent presence. I learned to resist him when I needed to, but I knew to let myself be overcome at the right moment. My honor came from the depths of my heart, and I accepted no guide but my conscience. All I wanted, you see, was his happiness; and for myself, to be considered a perfect wife."

OLD WOMAN: Stupid.

YOUNG WOMAN: I loved him.

OLD WOMAN: Stupid drivel.

YOUNG WOMAN: I loved him and I died for him.

OLD WOMAN: Died?

YOUNG WOMAN: I *tried.*

OLD WOMAN: But you *didn't.* Don't mix up, mutilate, pervert, disguise—

YOUNG WOMAN: I *did* taste death.

OLD WOMAN: And I *did* bring you back to life, I *tried* to make you taste a new life.

(*Pause. The YOUNG WOMAN picks up a blue bottle and pours oil on her hands. From now until the end of the play, she will massage all of the OLD WOMAN'S body, without leaving even the smallest spot of skin without oil.*)

OLD WOMAN: I like it when you touch me because I know you hate it. You've always hated it. I can still remember the first massage you gave me, you started with my feet. And you hated it! Now I make you do more. Do you hear the sound of skin pulling away from flesh, also? Now, as for me, I think it's kind of funny. (*Imitates the sound of skin pulling away from flesh.*) That oil is new.

YOUNG WOMAN: What?

OLD WOMAN: That oil is new.

YOUNG WOMAN: Yes. How did you know?

OLD WOMAN: By the ... smell.

YOUNG WOMAN: You have no sense of smell anymore.

OLD WOMAN: By the ... texture.

YOUNG WOMAN: You have no sense of touch anymore.

OLD WOMAN: By the sound, stupid. By the sound of your ring hitting the glass. And it's a different kind of glass. Blue. I can recognize the sound of Hector's ring hitting anything, of any color. For six months I've been hearing Hector's damn ring hitting the purple bottle. But you really should take off Hector's ring to give me my massage. It's not ... professional. You should take it off.

YOUNG WOMAN: No, never.

OLD WOMAN: My son was an imbecile, Andromache.

YOUNG WOMAN: No. He made me happy.

OLD WOMAN: The only happiness my son gave you was when he was sick. He gave you the chance to be a saint at his bedside, since he wouldn't let you be a demon between the sheets. Didn't you get bored, girl? From the beginning, the very beginning, when he came out from between my thighs, I knew I hadn't given birth to a good lover. He left the fleshy comfort of the uterus, to come into this world of thorns and products, without complaining, without trying to reclaim the parasitic condition of a satisfied fetus. He resigned himself immediately. "Grab onto the nipple!" and he grabbed on, bless him. He didn't grow teeth and nails until he was two years old. Actually, he never grew teeth and nails. He didn't cry at night, he never got anything but the most common illnesses. Just colic, and once in a while, once in a loooong while, diaper rash like any other brat. Nothing worthwhile. There was no way he could have made you happy. After all, you are a woman, right? (*Silence.*) Fine. I don't know if I'll be able to take the good story that I need to take. It's impossible to write good stories with you. Even less so happy endings. A whole lifetime trying. You are, quite frankly, insipid and boring. I'll go with my suitcase empty.

YOUNG WOMAN: What about my death? You. You wouldn't let me have a happy ending. You wouldn't let me die with him ...

OLD WOMAN: You know, you'll have to give back that story, too ...

YOUNG WOMAN: No, this one is mine, I don't have to give it back. It's mine, and it's the only one I have apart from you. This one explains me. And we'll keep it. We'll keep three stories. Just three. This story of mine would have been good if you had let me die, if you hadn't let me feel death. "Everything was set. The young woman hid in the bushes so that when she cut open her veins, the blind woman's damned ear would not hear."

OLD WOMAN: You see. My damned ear is not just a burden for me. "The blind old woman, from the parlor, heard the blood running from your wrist to the tips of your fingers and how it dripped to the ground and from the ground to the gutters. And through the gutters there was an unbearable sound of blood flowing through the skeleton of the house. The sound of a senseless death." And I saved you. Saved? (*Laughs.*) Is this the ending that you think explains us? A suicide for love? In any case, dear: the ending is predictable, meaningless, clichéd, backward, easy and weak ... or, in other words, it's not modern. You thought this ending would honor you, but you see, as time has passed, it degrades you. No one would ever rewrite your story, dear, no one would steal it from you. And if there are no thieves, there are no stories.

YOUNG WOMAN: Why? Why? Why should I be like you? Why should I be a woman like you, with fangs all over her body? Why can't someone die for a man, and especially, why can't one die with him? Why can't everyone just let me be a slave and victim of the man I love? Why do you let me be followed by a blind woman's gaze, at a time and in a way that are not the ones my conscience has chosen?

OLD WOMAN: Because conscience, a tranquil conscience, has nothing to do with happiness, dear ...

YOUNG WOMAN: I want to live off the happiness of the marble floor of my palace, scrubbed with a product that leaves it like a mirror. And for that floor to extend like a carpet that I spread before my husband to lead him to my bed. Like Andromache. And, like Ruth, at night I want to pull the blanket away from my husband's feet and stretch out and wait for him to tell me what he wants ...

OLD WOMAN: Speaking of blankets, it might get cold. Put my shawl in the suitcase.

YOUNG WOMAN: You don't need a suitcase! I already told you, you don't need a suitcase! You want a happy ending, old woman? You want a happy one?

OLD WOMAN: It will get cold. Put my shawl in the suitcase, dear.

YOUNG WOMAN: Don't call me "dear." Enough. (*Pause.*) Call me Draupadi.

OLD WOMAN: It will get cold. My shawl.

(*Silence. The YOUNG WOMAN pours more oil onto her hands. She coats the OLD WOMAN's genitals.*)

OLD WOMAN: Don't you hate it? This is really a very thorough massage, dear. You've never tried so hard. A new technique? Don't you hate it?

YOUNG WOMAN: No.

OLD WOMAN: Pity. Are you afraid? Aren't you afraid of the teeth?

YOUNG WOMAN: You won't need the shawl there. It doesn't get cold. It's always the same temperature, about eighty degrees. And you know what? You don't sweat. You can wear the same dress for as long as you want. You don't need another one.

OLD WOMAN: A white one.

YOUNG WOMAN: A white one. Whatever you want. It doesn't get dirty. The air is pure, not like here. You'll be fine. Have I mentioned that they clean the toilet inside and out, every day?

OLD WOMAN: Maybe twice a day?

YOUNG WOMAN: It might even be three times. Inside and out.

(*Silence.*)

OLD WOMAN: Don't cry. Why are you crying? I told you not to cry. I can't stand it when you cry, or when you keep crying silently inside. Isn't it enough that I have to hear, day after day, how my body is falling apart? Then on top of that I have to hear all your body's moods? Silence!

(*Silence.*)

YOUNG WOMAN: What's wrong? You're shaking ...

OLD WOMAN: I hear a sound ...

YOUNG WOMAN: What does it sound like?

OLD WOMAN: You know I won't be able to describe it, curse you ... Be quiet ... I don't even recognize it ...

YOUNG WOMAN: The cat ...?

OLD WOMAN: Shhh! ... no ... a new sound ... (*Pause.*) I'm afraid ...

YOUNG WOMAN: ... are they coming ...? Are they close? Miles? Feet?

OLD WOMAN: I'm afraid. Feet. Yes. Call me ... Chandra ... or whatever the hell you call me. Quickly ... call me Chandra.

YOUNG WOMAN: No! (*Pause.*) So soon? No. There's still time.

OLD WOMAN: No. Come on, tell me your stupid damn story. (*Pause.*) Come on, Draupadi.

(*Pause.*)

YOUNG WOMAN: Draupadi was the happiest woman in the world on her wedding day. Her husband was poor, but he had lips on his arms and kisses hidden behind his ears, under his armpits, between his toes ... and Draupadi enjoyed looking for them, at all hours. But what the young wife liked best was that her husband existed, and she gave herself up to him. Their poverty forced them to go live with the groom's mother, who was a widow with a beautiful name: Chandra.

Chandra was good and respectful to Draupadi. She had just one defect: she existed; and that old woman existed a lot. For Chandra to exist meant that Draupadi also existed; and Draupadi wanted *him* to be the only one that existed.

But, one unhappy day, her husband died. With that emptiness, Chandra's presence multiplied and spread throughout the house.

Then, Draupadi decided to kill her mother-in-law.

In the town there was a well-known old herbalist, who the townspeople relied on whenever their hearts ached for some reason. Draupadi stole her miserable dowry and went to get the herbalist to recommend her a poison.

"What is the motive for the murder? Emotional? Business? Political?" the old man asked after hearing Draupadi's request.

The young woman didn't really know how to answer him. It had never occurred to her that there could be a motive for killing beyond the wish to make someone disappear. But since what ached was her heart, she decided that the murder was probably of the emotional kind.

The herbalist went to one of the shelves and showed her three bottles of three different colors. Caressing the green bottle, he said:

"This one is Berzolas oil. It kills instantly. Apply it to the earlobes, the lips, the palm of the hand, or the genitals. It is frequently used by the young, who don't doubt for a moment that what they feel at the time is what they feel their whole lives. They use it on their lover, their parents, their friends and their teachers indiscriminately; all of them are presumably victims of momentary passions. This oil has an antidote. But it must be applied within forty-five seconds. The antidote, naturally, is given free when Berzolas oil is bought, even if the customer takes it as an insult to the seriousness of their intentions. And the antidote is used with as much passion and more frequently than you would think. It's used nearly ninety-six percent of the time, in a reflex that's surprisingly agile. The other four percent don't use it, but not out of lack of desire or of reflexes. Sometimes, more often than we would like, it turns out that there's something wrong with the cap, and it can't be opened in time. These things happen."

(The OLD WOMAN smiles.)

"This is Florence oil," he said, showing her the blue bottle. "Florence oil takes about twenty minutes to take effect. It is usually used by friends, family members or lovers who figure that they will need about twenty minutes to tell their loved one everything they haven't been able to say in the years of their relationship. Those who only open their heart before a deathbed. When you hear a murderer say about his victim `It's a shame, I would have liked to tell them so many things!,' they must not have known about Florence oil. It is applied as a full-body massage, without leaving the smallest spot of skin without oil. When the last pore of skin is covered by the ointment and the last minute runs out, the person will die."

The old herbalist picked up the last flask, a purple one.

"And this oil is Cercis Siliquastrum, the tree of love or of Judas. It kills very slowly, little by little with betrayal. It consumes the victim slowly, the way nature does, and it is usually used by customers who have had a life filled with loss that they shared with the person in question. The poison acts in the same way that life has acted on the person's spirit, which is why it is called of love and Judas, because the caress brings betrayal, because that which gives you life, now gives you death. The profile of the customer who uses it is simple and merciless, the way nature is; someone who does not love exceptional stories. It is applied by giving gentle massages to the upper and lower limbs. These two oils *(Pause.)* have no antidote. Oh, and don't worry; needless to say, they're harmless on the skin of the murderer."

OLD WOMAN: Even though Draupadi wanted to free herself quickly from the Presence, she couldn't stand the idea of touching the old woman's whole body without leaving any bare spots. She imagined massaging the old woman's genitals and was afraid. *(The YOUNG WOMAN pauses for a few seconds. She looks at the OLD WOMAN strangely. Then she sadly continues the massage.)* She didn't know why, but she imagined the old woman would have teeth between her legs. She didn't know why. Maybe Draupadi had stolen it from some book. So she passed over the Florence oil. And more and more, the oil of Cercis Siliquastrum matched the characteristics of their relationship.

YOUNG WOMAN: How do you know this story? It's mine. I dreamed it.

OLD WOMAN: I can hear your dreams ... and your wishes.

YOUNG WOMAN: Why didn't you ever tell me? Why did you let me—

OLD WOMAN: Because it's a good story. (*Pause.*) I'll be full when I go. Come on. Finish, it's getting late: "She got home and began to massage—"

YOUNG WOMAN: "Chandra's feet. Chandra was not surprised by Draupadi's generosity. Every day Chandra was thrilled to receive Draupadi's caresses, and every day Chandra would give Draupadi an old story, a story of love or loss that had to do with the two of them. Draupadi would caress that skin like paper, anguishing because she could hear how it pulled away from the flesh, she felt the muscles coming apart under her palms; but every day, she felt more and more desire to caress Chandra. The old woman was consumed slowly, her hair fell out in handfuls, she could feel the bones breaking down, how her eyes rolled back in their sockets, how her teeth fell out of her gums. All those absences further reinforced that presence that, now, strangely, she loved."

OLD WOMAN: "That morning, very early, before her mother-in-law woke up, Draupadi secretly slipped out of her house and went to the herbalist and bought Florence oil, the oil that killed in twenty minutes. She couldn't think of any other way to end the old woman's suffering and the suffering of her own spirit. That oil would allow her, at the same time, to explain for the last time the old stories and tales of love and loss that Chandra had taught her to appropriate." (*Pause.*) They're here.

(*The OLD WOMAN looks off into the distance. The YOUNG WOMAN dresses her in a white dress.*)

YOUNG WOMAN: And during that last massage, with traces of skin under her nails and hair in her pockets, Draupadi described the landscape of death to Chandra, just as she remembered it from when she had felt death long ago.

OLD WOMAN: You were right. It has a garden, with the damn gravel. But I can't hear it.

(*Pause.*)

YOUNG WOMAN: Maybe, from being with the fireflies so much, the gravel has learned to express itself with words of light.

OLD WOMAN: Drivel. (*Pause.*) And my God! Look at old Agnes's cat, he's soaked. Now he's meowing in silence, with his lungs full of water. Will you tell Agnes not to look for him anymore? (*Laughs.*)

YOUNG WOMAN: I'm sorry.

OLD WOMAN: Don't be sorry. It will take me a while to get used to it, but I'm going to like it. It's very quiet.

YOUNG WOMAN: No. That's not what's bothering me. It's beautiful and clichéd to kill you with caresses. No. I'm just sorry that I tricked you: I don't know if they clean the toilet, inside and out ...

OLD WOMAN: And that stuff about the cookies in the middle of the afternoon?

YOUNG WOMAN: I don't know that either. I'm sorry.

OLD WOMAN: It's not your fault, I didn't let you get past the threshold. Actually, I'm happier than ever that I didn't let you enter. You have written a good story. Everything makes sense, now. It's a good one.

YOUNG WOMAN: The men with the labcoats the color of sand, do you see them?

OLD WOMAN: Yes, men with labcoats the color of sand, exactly, and extra wings on the buildings, and a lot of old people, girl. Disgusting. Just what I figured ... (*Pause.*) No, look over there, I see a child, poor thing, so little and so alone, with scabs all over ... (*Pause. Looks at the YOUNG WOMAN.*) Do you think that they'll write this story, really write it?

YOUNG WOMAN: Maybe someone, someday, will learn to describe in words the sound of stories.

OLD WOMAN: What? I can't hear you, dear. Don't stop touching me ... (*In a murmur, looking into the distance.*) A single room, please.

BLACKOUT

El color del gos quan fuig (*Killing Time*), Sala Beckett,
Barcelona, 1997. Directed by Beth Escudé i Gallès.

Itziar Ortega and Beatriz Fernández in *Pullus (Killing Time)*, Sala Galileo, Madrid. September 2001, dir. Adolfo Simón. Photo: Benito Lorenzo.

KEEPING IN TOUCH
(***La lladre i la Sra Guix***)

Translated from the Catalan

by

Janet DeCesaris

La lladre i la Sra Guix (*Keeping in Touch*) was originally written as a radio play and was first aired in 1999 on Catalunya Ràdio in the series "Els espais dramàtics," directed by Dolors Martínez.

CHARACTERS

OLD WOMAN
YOUNG WOMAN
MAN

Note on music used in the text:
Nicola Matteis (?-1714?) was a violinist-composer born in Naples, Italy. He moved to England circa 1672, and did most of his work there. Besides playing and teaching violin and guitar, he is best known for composing the *Ayres for the Violin*, which include "Diverse bizzarie Sopra la Vecchia Sarabanda o pu Ciaccona." This piece is written in four parts: violin, viola da gamba, recorder, and theorbo. The playwright feels that this particular piece, and the contrast between the cell phone and the orchestra recording, are vital to the work.

B.M.K.

SCENE 1

Two spaces. A street and a house. In the street, the OLD WOMAN enters a telephone booth. She puts a coin in the slot and dials a number. After a few seconds, we hear the silly melody of a cell phone that plays the first line of "Diverse Bizzarie sopra la Vecchia Sarabanda o pu Ciaccona" by Nicola Matteis. The YOUNG WOMAN, at home, answers.

YOUNG WOMAN: Who is it?

OLD WOMAN (*Angrily*): What do you mean "Who is it"? Who are *you*?

(*Silence.*)

I am the owner of the cell phone you're holding. I am the owner of the papers you're holding. And of the handbag you're holding.

(*Noise as if to hang up.*)

No, please, don't hang up. Damn it. (*The OLD WOMAN goes through her coat pockets. She swears.*) She's cleaned me out. (*The OLD WOMAN opens the door to the booth and talks to someone who is waiting to make a call. She speaks with a soft, pleading voice.*) Excuse me, young man, would you be kind enough to lend me some money to call my daughter? My handbag was just stolen and I don't have any money on me. I was so scared there for a minute. I'm not in good health. I have a heart condition, you know? My pills were in my bag. I have to call my daughter so she can come get me. I don't even have my senior citizen card for the bus. (*Pause. She is given a coin.*) Thank you very much. I'll be done in a minute.

(*She closes the door to the booth again. She dials. The cell phone rings again. The YOUNG WOMAN takes a while to answer.*)

Come on, you fool, answer, answer.

(*The YOUNG WOMAN answers the phone.*)

Listen, don't you hang up on me. I only have one coin and this is important. I don't have any intention of reporting you. You can keep the money, you can keep the make-up, it's all good brands. Do you like to wear make-up?

(*Silence.*)

You can keep the cell phone too, if you want, I don't really understand how to use it very well. But please listen, in the little inside pocket you'll find a picture. It's important to me. Could you send it to me at the address in my wallet?

YOUNG WOMAN: I don't know how to write.

OLD WOMAN: Oh, damn.

(*Pause.*)

YOUNG WOMAN: But I can ask my son to do it. He's four. He doesn't know how to write very well. But he knows how to imitate letters.

OLD WOMAN: Not exactly the most reliable way but okay, it'll do. I'd appreciate it. (*Pause.*) I never had time to have children. What's his name?

(*Silence.*)

Okay, I understand. It doesn't matter. I just wanted to get the picture back somehow. If I were your age, I would trust my memory and you could keep that piece of paper. But that's not the case. I think you owe me this much, since you cleaned me out.

YOUNG WOMAN: I don't owe anything to anyone.

OLD WOMAN: Of course not, of course not. But, will you do it, please? I have other pictures of my father, but none like that one. It's difficult for people to look like themselves in a photograph. And here he does. The girl hanging around his neck, who's rubbing her nose on his cheek, is me. Well, it's not me now. It was me. I looked like that then: a young woman with a future. A long road ahead of me. The picture was taken at the station precisely because I was on my way to London. Now I'm not what I promised to be, of course. Just like he wasn't at the moment my mother pressed the camera shutter.

YOUNG WOMAN: His name is Hassan. My son is named Hassan.

(*Pause.*)

OLD WOMAN: Nice. That's a fine name. Well, can I trust you to send it to me?

(*Silence.*)

Hey, are you there? Will you do it?

YOUNG WOMAN: Call me again at another time. Next week.

OLD WOMAN: What? What did you say?

YOUNG WOMAN: You'll ask about my son. And, if you remember, about my mother. "How was your day today?" is a good question, too. I'll talk to you about your picture. I'll keep it.

OLD WOMAN: That's ridiculous. Well, it was already ridiculous when you answered the phone you had just stolen.

YOUNG WOMAN: I'll describe the picture to you.

OLD WOMAN: What? You have to describe it to me? Come on, let's stop fooling around and tell Abdul to imitate the letters of—

YOUNG WOMAN: The picture must be important to you. Don't worry. I will describe it to you. And I will be precise.

OLD WOMAN: But it won't be the same!

YOUNG WOMAN: No, it won't.

(*She hangs up.*)

OLD WOMAN: Hey, hey, hello ...

(*The "Diverse Bizzarie sopra la Vecchia Sarabanda o pu Ciaccona" by Nicola Matteis, this time an orchestra recording, sounds in the background.*)

SCENE II

The OLD WOMAN makes a telephone call. The YOUNG WOMAN is standing in line in an office. She answers the phone.

OLD WOMAN: Did I get you at a bad time? Where are you?

YOUNG WOMAN: I'm standing in line.

OLD WOMAN: Again? What kind of line?

YOUNG WOMAN: A line to get in another line. (*Pause. Sound of a buzzer indicating the next turn.*) There are only five people ahead of me.

OLD WOMAN: You'll get it. With a child they'll let you stay for sure. By the way, how is ... Ali? (*Pause.*) And your mother? How is it going these days?

YOUNG WOMAN: You are so kind to ask. I called my mother today. She cried again. Mothers cry a lot, back home.

(*Silence.*)

OLD WOMAN: Call her as often as you want.

YOUNG WOMAN: All right.

OLD WOMAN: No. Really. You didn't spend too much last month. I can afford it.

YOUNG WOMAN: Yesterday I got $19.95. Just what that little table I had told you about cost. I bought it first thing this morning. Isn't it funny that there was exactly $19.95 in that old woman's handbag? Not a cent more. Just what a little dream costs. (*The buzzer indicating the next turn sounds again.*) There are only four people ahead of me.

OLD WOMAN: Do you have it with you?

YOUNG WOMAN (*Abruptly, in an unfriendly tone*): I'm not finished yet. (*Pause. She switches to a nice tone.*) The table has a small scratch on it; that's why it was so cheap. It looks very nice in the living room. I'm going to cover it with a sheet so that Hassan doesn't get crayon all over it. Hassan likes to draw.

OLD WOMAN: Of course. (*Pause.*) Do you have the picture with you?

YOUNG WOMAN (*Dryly*): Yes. (*The buzzer sounds again. Pause.*) She really held on tight, you know? I had to yank hard. She must have torn her stockings. She might have even skinned her knees. I don't know because I don't usually turn around. I have her medical insurance card. I'll send it to her. Hassan has very good writing. And her ID. Or perhaps I'll go see her. I will tell her that I used her money to buy a little blue table with a bouquet of flowers on each corner. I will ask her for the name of the flowers. I will ask her to look it up in her books. She looked like someone who would have a lot of books about plants. That way I can teach Hassan the names of the flowers. Perhaps she will ask for my telephone number. Perhaps she will call to ask about my mother and my little boy. She'll probably sound more believable than you do. She may scold me for what I do. Do you think she would think it's all right for me to knock old ladies down on the sidewalk—?

OLD WOMAN: You can settle that question with your God. Don't get me involved here. (*The buzzer sounds again.*) Come on. Describe.

YOUNG WOMAN (*Mechanically*): A man to the left, about age sixty, going on seventy. A happy girl is hugging him. She's a bit over thirty. Lots of curly hair that contrasts with the man's, who has almost none. In my country they would be considered rich. But here they're middle class. A train station in the background. A big one. You can imagine a high ceiling.

OLD WOMAN: Don't tell me what you can imagine, tell me what you see. Exactly what you see.

YOUNG WOMAN: A hug. Only a hug.

OLD WOMAN: That's not true. There's one more thing.

YOUNG WOMAN: No. Only a hug.

(*The buzzer sounds again.*)

OLD WOMAN: I can't remember who took the picture. We're at the station, aren't we? Where were we going, anyway? To Paris? To Cologne?

YOUNG WOMAN: I don't think it matters. I have to go now. It's my turn. (*She hangs up. Speaking to someone else.*) For a residence permit.

MAN: Window twelve.

(Sound of "Diverse Bizzarie..." by Matteis, as played by an orchestra.)

A factory. The cell phone rings. The YOUNG WOMAN answers it.

YOUNG WOMAN (*Speaking over the noise of machines.*) Hello. Hello. Hang on. I can't hear you. (*Speaking to someone else.*) Could you take a look at the bottle caps? I don't think they fit right. Everything has worked fine all morning. To get the cap to fit right you do this. (*Noise.*) With the piston. It's very easy. Tragically easy. It's my fiancé. He gets angry because I work. This'll only take a minute. I'll do your half hour for you and that way you can leave early. Thanks a lot.

(*She moves away from the machine. Speaking to the OLD WOMAN, on the telephone.*)

I can talk now.

OLD WOMAN: Just tell me where he's looking.

YOUNG WOMAN: Aren't you going to ask me anything?

OLD WOMAN: I asked you the questions before. Right after you answered the phone. I don't need to repeat them. You already know the questions.

YOUNG WOMAN: I haven't heard them. I was next to the machine.

OLD WOMAN: That's not my problem. I've kept my part of the bargain. You never said I would have to repeat the questions.

YOUNG WOMAN: Why are you so stupid? Okay. Answering that question isn't part of the deal we had, either, is it?

OLD WOMAN: Precisely.

YOUNG WOMAN: Okay, you bitter old hag. I'm not going to change you at this point. You could add, just this once, "How's your job going?" You know I got the job, don't you?

OLD WOMAN: Congratulations. (*Dryly, and all at once.*) How is your mother? And Muhammad? How was your day today?

YOUNG WOMAN: How nice of you to ask. I haven't called my mother. Last week she didn't even recognize me. I had to tell her that I was her daughter, although I knew that wasn't the most important point. (*Silence.*) Hassan has grown a lot. He has a friend at school now. When I picked him up at school, I saw how a younger boy smiled at him. If he hadn't had both hands occupied—his mother was holding one and a toy truck was in the other—he surely would have waved at Hassan from a distance. My new job? It's fine, thank you. I've been lucky.

OLD WOMAN: You'll be able to buy many flowered tables. (*Silence.*) They're probably freesia buds. What you described sounds like freesia.

YOUNG WOMAN: Freesia?

OLD WOMAN: I'm not absolutely positive.

YOUNG WOMAN: Freesias are fine. Thank you for remembering to look it up after all this time.

OLD WOMAN: I didn't look it up. I don't have any books about plants at home. I don't like plants. They create work and tie you down. And then they thank you by reminding you of how everything comes to an end. It was by chance. Okay. It's my turn now.

YOUNG WOMAN: Yes. A man on the left, sixty-some years old, going on seventy ...

OLD WOMAN: Tell me which direction he's looking in.

YOUNG WOMAN: The direction he's always looked in. Pictures don't change. They never betray you.

OLD WOMAN: But my memory does. Please.

YOUNG WOMAN: The man's eyes seem to be looking at something in the distance. Nonetheless, he is looking inwards. He is no longer able to see anything beyond himself. He is looking at the path the hug has taken to his belly. The girl is looking at the camera and smiling, sure that she will hug him again when she comes back from her trip. It's the camera lens that is rather unsure. (*The machine noise ceases.*) The man has his hands in his pockets and his pants have slid down so that we can see his whole belly covered by a linen shirt. He's not hugging the girl; she does the hugging for both of them. The man lets himself be loved, but there's an unpleasant quality, a touch of excess pride in the last stretch of his life. The metaphor of the station, the trip, betray only her, as she still knows nothing. You can see that in her one eye that is looking quite innocently at the camera. And the other eye, which like her nose appears ridiculous as it rubs against her friend's dry cheek, does not penetrate the skin. She is not looking inwards, she is not thinking, she is not hurt. Am I being precise enough?

OLD WOMAN: Yes.

YOUNG WOMAN: A sweet trembling is discreetly creeping up the girl's back, bone by bone.

OLD WOMAN: You can see the girl's back? From what I recall, both of them were looking at the camera.

YOUNG WOMAN: Yes, but this is a strange picture indeed. We can see her back. Even though the edge of the picture cuts them off at the thighs, we can see their toes. His are stuck to the ground, as if they had suction cups. Hers are acting crazy, one on top of another, fighting to occupy more space in her shoes.

OLD WOMAN: Yes, I remember. Go on.

YOUNG WOMAN: You can also see a sound in the picture. (*A train whistle sounds.*) A smell. Is it after-shave? (*The bustle of an old train station gets louder and louder.*) Some words, but nothing important. Some laughs. (*We hear the loudspeaker announcing the departure of a train. The YOUNG WOMAN, speaking in a different voice.*) "Honey, look at the camera."

OLD WOMAN: That's enough pictures. I'm going to miss it. This is the last one, okay, Mom? What a pain!

(*A man laughs.*)

YOUNG WOMAN: "Yes. This is the last one."

(*Silence.*)

OLD WOMAN: That was the last time I saw him. He didn't make it through the operation they had hidden from me.

(*The bustle of the train station becomes louder. It then becomes fainter as we hear the orchestra recording of Matteis's music in the background.*)

SCENE IV

The OLD WOMAN's wall phone rings. Two spaces: the OLD WOMAN's house and a police station.)

OLD WOMAN: Yes, speaking.

MAN: I'm calling from the local police station. We've located a handbag with some documents that have your name on them. Were you robbed recently?

OLD WOMAN: I can't recall.

MAN: It may have been some time ago. This was found in an abandoned building that's going to be demolished. From the looks of the bag I'd say it was left there some time ago. It's beige. There are keys, some make-up ...

(Pause.)

OLD WOMAN: Maybe it is mine. Could you please look in the inside pocket? There should be a picture there.

(The MAN fishes around in the purse.)

MAN: I'm sorry, it's not here. The roof of the building had caved in. The bag was out in the rain. There are bits of paper everywhere, but you can't tell what they are. I'm sorry. There's no photograph.

OLD WOMAN: Don't be sorry. Someone must have taken it.

MAN: Do you want us to send it to you? Just a minute. An old photograph. In very bad shape. Yes, I have it. I think there's a man and—

OLD WOMAN (*Expressing disappointment*): Yes, yes. That's right. It was a few years ago.

MAN: Do you want us to send you the handbag?

OLD WOMAN: No. It's not necessary. I had the documents redone and the locks changed.

MAN: Wise decision. You have to be extra careful in these cases. Do you want to stop by and pick up the picture?

OLD WOMAN (*Passionately*): Please. (*Pause. She changes her tone of voice.*) No. It's not necessary. Don't bother. Thank you for calling.

MAN: That's our job, ma'am. Good-bye.

(*The OLD WOMAN hangs up. Silence. She places a phone call. The silly melody of the cell phone. The YOUNG WOMAN answers.*)

OLD WOMAN: Have you had a good day today? What's Hassan up to? Tell me about the hug.

(*The orchestra recording of "Diverse Bizzarie..." by Nicola Matteis.*)

THE END

CRITICAL REACTION TO THE PLAYS

Killing Time "presents the relationship between two women, one young and the other old, who are tied by family and biography.... Incapable of grasping their own existence, they have dedicated their lives to stealing transcribed stories that have to do with them and their relationship.... Only thus can they explain and give sense to the `lightness of being.'"

> Sección Espectáculos
> *ABC Cataluña* (21 May 1997)

"Cruelty, tenderness, humor and tragedy in the relationship established by two women: a daughter and mother-in-law united beyond the man who `married' them. They tell their story, the common tale and the personal one, through other mothers and daughters-in-law from the Bible (Naomi and Ruth) and mythology (Hecuba and Andromache)."

> Nuria Cuadrado
> *El Mundo* (21 May 1997)

"Something in the story made me go on reading; my intuition said that an enigma was hidden behind the words and I had to discover it. I reached the last page with the sensation of not knowing what really was happening between these two women, and yet I could not stop thinking about them. Unwittingly, I was being poisoned, I was falling in love with a story I did not understand but that left me disconcerted."

> Adolfo Simón
> *ADE Teatro* (July-Sept. 2001)

Whether the Old Woman's death is "an act of euthanasia or a homicide, or an ambiguous act that cannot easily be explained, both the act and the moment are profoundly human and moving."

> Candyce Leonard
> *Nuevos Manantiales* (Ottawa: GIROL, 2001)

CRITICAL REACTIONS TO THE PLAY

ABOUT THE TRANSLATORS

Janet DeCesaris first became interested in translation while an undergraduate at Georgetown University, where she obtained a B.S. degree in language and linguistics. She then went on to earn two M.A. degrees and a Ph.D. at Indiana University-Bloomington. After teaching at Rutgers University in the mid-1980s, she moved to Catalonia. She currently is Associate Professor of Translation and Interpreting at Pompeu Fabra University in Barcelona, and her research interests include lexicography, translation, and linguistics. She is the national coordinator for the translation panel of the *Asociación Española de Lingüística Aplicada* and the secretary of the newly created *Asociación Española de Lexicografía*. This is her second translation for the ESTRENO Plays series.

Bethany M. Korp first studied translation at the Universitat de València in Valencia, Spain. She went on to take more classes in translation as part of her B.A. in Spanish from the College of William & Mary. In 2001, she won the American Foundation for Translation and Interpretation's First Annual Scholarship in Literary Translation. She completed her M.A. in Spanish translation at Rutgers, the State University of New Jersey, in 2002. She is accredited by the American Translators Association in Spanish-English translation and works as a freelance Spanish-English translator and interpreter, and also teaches translation and medical interpretation. She recently translated César Aira's novella *Cómo me hice monja* (*How I Became a Nun*) into English. *Killing Time* is her first published literary translation, her first work from Catalan to English, and her first for ESTRENO Plays.

44

ACKNOWLEDGEMENTS

The translator would like to thank the editor of the ESTRENO series, Phyllis Zatlin, and the assistant editor of this play, Bethany M. Korp, for their helpful comments. Comments by the play's author, Beth Escudé i Gallès, also helped to clarify several points. I am sure that this translation has improved as a result of their careful reading.

Janet DeCesaris

The translator would like to thank Phyllis Zatlin for this opportunity and for her helpful suggestions. She would also like to thank Beth Escudé i Gallès for her willingness to help and her openness to suggestions, as well as for having written a work that was such a joy (and a challenge) to translate. Finally, a special thank you to the people of Valencia, Spain, for teaching her their beautiful language. *Moltes gràcies i una forta abraçada.*

Bethany M. Korp

On behalf of ESTRENO Plays, I express our appreciation to the Institució de les Lletres Catalanes of the Departament de Cultura, Generalitat de Catalunya for their generous support of this edition. I am especially grateful to Iolanda Pelegri for her invaluable advice and encouragement and, of course, to Beth Escudé i Gallès, who patiently answered our many questions and took an active role in the creation of these translations. Both Janet DeCesaris and Bethany Korp participated in this project beyond the normal function of translators: Janet in the preparation of our initial proposal to the Institució and Bethany as assistant editor of this volume. The timely publication of this edition owes much to Bethany's perceptive attention to details of language and culture and her conscientious pursuit of solutions. My thanks as well to Kerri Allen for her usual careful and insightful reading of the final manuscript and her always welcome suggestions on matters of theatrical language and style, and to Nydia Otero for her boundless patience in readying the text for the press.

Phyllis Zatlin
Editor

ESTRENO: CONTEMPORARY SPANISH PLAYS SERIES

No. 1   Jaime Salom: *Bonfire at Dawn* *(Una hoguera al amanecer)*
Translated by Phyllis Zatlin. 1992.
ISBN: 0-9631212-0-0

No. 2   José López Rubio: *In August We Play the Pyrenees* *(Celos del aire)*
Translated by Marion Peter Holt. 1992.
ISBN: 0-9631212-1-9

No. 3   Ramón del Valle-Inclán: *Savage Acts: Four Plays* (*Ligazón, La rosa de papel, La cabeza del Bautista, Sacrilegio*)
Translated by Robert Lima. 1993.
ISBN: 0-9631212-2-7

No. 4   Antonio Gala: *The Bells of Orleans* (*Los buenos días perdidos*)
Translated by Edward Borsoi. 1993.
ISBN: 0-9631212-3-5

No. 5   Antonio Buero-Vallejo: *The Music Window* *(Música cercana)*
Translated by Marion Peter Holt. 1994.
ISBN: 0-9631212-4-3

No. 6   Paloma Pedrero: *Parting Gestures with A Night in the Subway* (*El color de agosto, La noche dividida, Resguardo personal, Solos esta noche*)
Translated by Phyllis Zatlin. Revised edition. 1999.
ISBN: 1-888463-06-6

No. 7   Ana Diosdado: *Yours for the Asking* (*Usted también podrá disfrutar de ella*)
Translated by Patricia W. O'Connor. 1995.
ISBN: 0-9631212-6-X

No. 8   Manuel Martínez Mediero: *A Love Too Beautiful* (*Juana del amor hermoso*)
Translated by Hazel Cazorla. 1995.
ISBN: 0-9631212-7-8

No. 9   Alfonso Vallejo: *Train to Kiu* *(El cero transparente)*
Translated by H. Rick Hite. 1996.
ISBN: 0-9631212-8-6

ORDER INFORMATION

List price, nos. 1-11: $6; revised ed. no. 6 and nos. 12-23, $8.
Shipping and handling for one or two volumes, $1.25 each.
Free postage on orders of three or more volumes.
Special price for complete set of 23 volumes, $110

Make checks payable to ESTRENO Plays and send to:

ESTRENO Plays
Dept. of Spanish & Portuguese, FAS
Rutgers, The State University of New Jersey
105 George Street
New Brunswick, NJ 08901-1414 USA

For information on discounts available to bookstores, contact:

FAX: 1-732/ 932-9837
Phone: 1-732/932-9412x25
E-mail: ESTRPLAY@rci.rutgers.edu

VISIT OUR WEB PAGE:

www.rci.rutgers.edu/~estrplay/webpage.html